Let's take a trip
out in space.
3...2...1...Blast off!

1

The Earth looks different from up here, doesn't it?

This is our Moon.
It moves around the Earth.

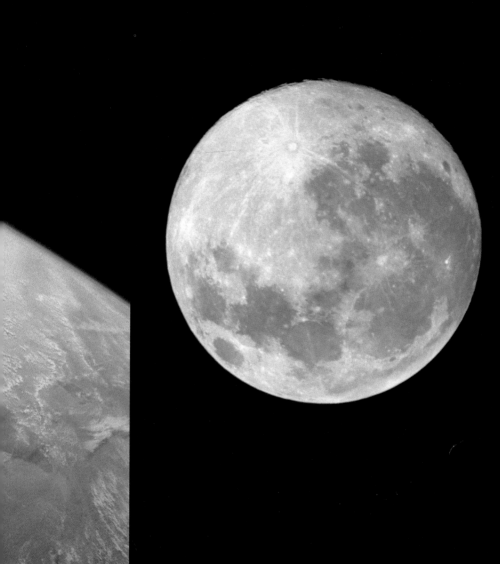

This is the Sun.

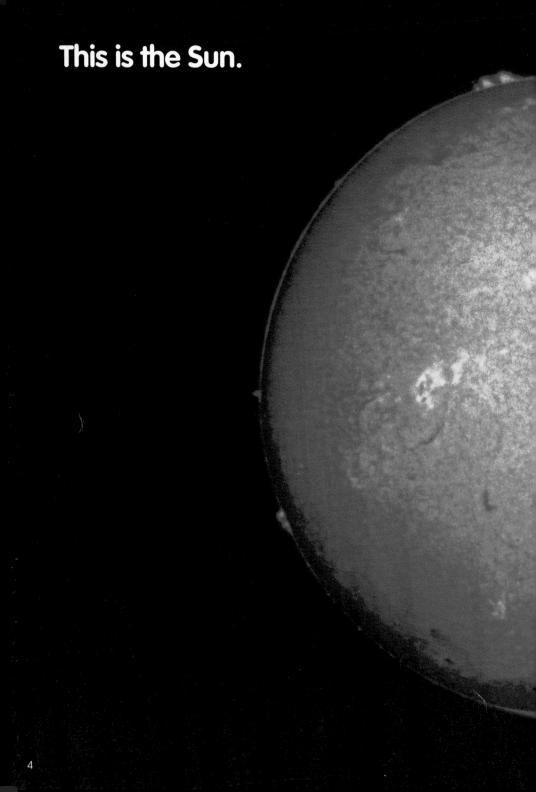

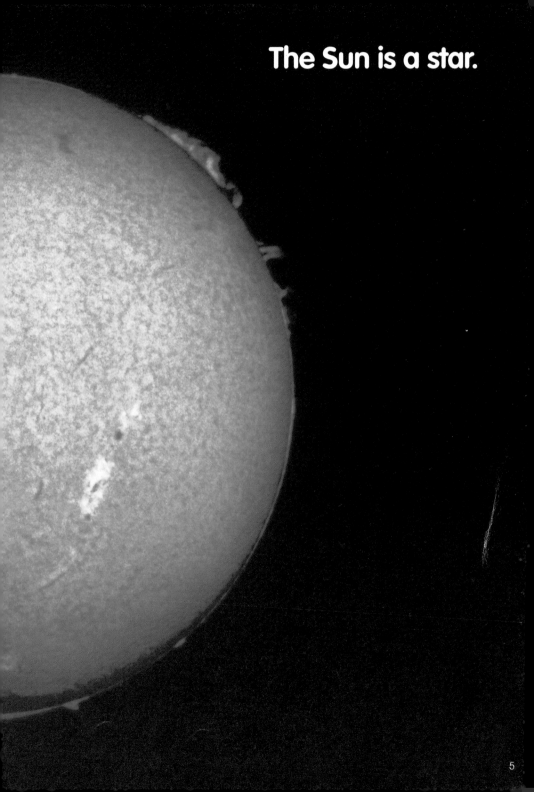

The Sun is a star.

Nine planets move around the Sun.

Mercury is the closest. Then Venus.

Mercury

Venus

Earth is the third planet from the Sun.

We pass Mars.

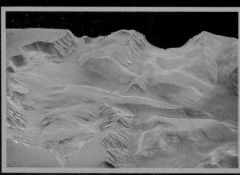

Look at its canyons!

We pass Jupiter.

Look at its giant red spot!

We pass Saturn.
Wow! Look at those rings!

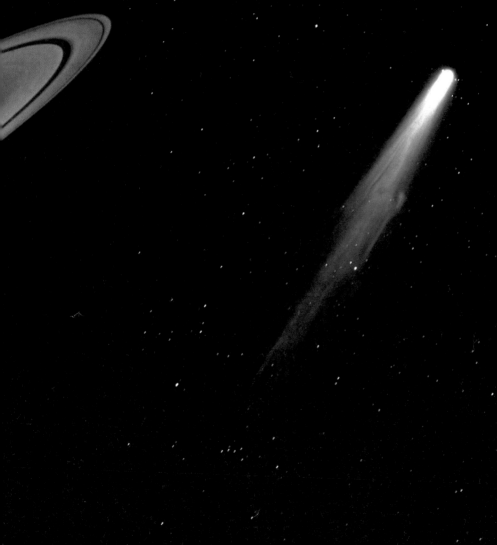

Look over there!
A comet is whizzing by.

We pass Uranus and Neptune.

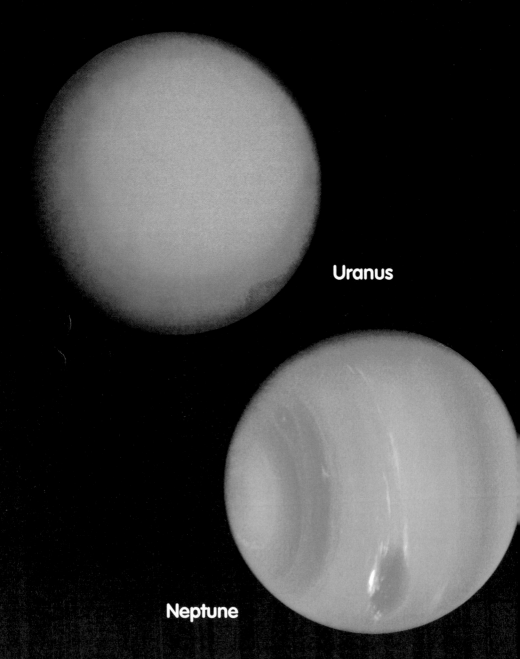

Uranus

Neptune

And, finally, we pass Pluto. Pluto is the last and smallest planet in our solar system.

Pluto

What else is out in space?
Lots of stars and galaxies!

Spiral Galaxy

Andromeda Galaxy

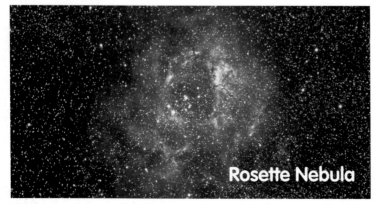

Rosette Nebula

Our galaxy is called the Milky Way.

Now we're back on planet Earth. It's great to be home.